Published by Creative Education
123 South Broad Street, Mankato, Minnesota 56001
Creative Education is an imprint of The Creative Company

Designed by Stephanie Blumenthal
Production Design by Rose Preble

Photographs by Derek Fell

Library of Congress Cataloging-in-Publication Data

Fell, Derek
Cacti / by Derek Fell
p. cm. — (Let's Investigate)
Includes glossary and index
Summary: Describes the history and development of cacti,
different species, their habitats, and some of their uses.
ISBN 1-58341-000-7
1. Cactus—Juvenile literature. [1.Cactus.] I. Title. II. Series.
III. Series: Let's Investigate (Mankato, Minn.)
QK495.C11F44   1999
583'56—dc21   99-11609

First edition

2 4 6 8 9 7 5 3 1

CACTI

DEREK FELL

Creative ◖ Education

CACTUS
GARDEN

The Huntington Botanical Garden, near Los Angeles, California, features the largest collection of cacti in the world.

Right, the Huntington Botanical Garden Above, some cacti resemble stones

Many kinds of plants cover the earth, from the Arctic Circle to the Antarctic, growing in a wide range of climatic conditions (from seering desert heat to freezing temperatures). The shape of a plant, its root structure, its flower form and leaf type all aid in a plant's ability to survive in a particular part of our planet. Cacti have adapted in all of these ways to survive in hot, dry deserts as well as tropical rain forests.

CACTUS
RELATIVE

Succulents are relatives of cacti; they have swollen stems and leaves suited for storing water and surviving long periods of dry weather.

CACTUS
GARDEN

The Huntington Botanical Garden, near Los Angeles, California, features the largest collection of cacti in the world.

Prickly pear cacti

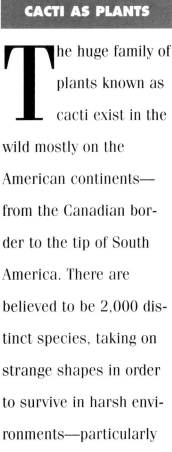

CACTI AS PLANTS

The huge family of plants known as cacti exist in the wild mostly on the American continents—from the Canadian border to the tip of South America. There are believed to be 2,000 distinct species, taking on strange shapes in order to survive in harsh environments—particularly deserts. Typically, cacti are barrel-shaped to store water during dry spells, and they are covered in sharp spines to protect themselves from **foraging** animals such as deer.

They generally lack leaves to reduce moisture loss. These desert cacti thrive in open, dry, sunny locations where little else is capable of growing. Indeed, if they are subjected to too much moisture they will easily die. Some are as small as pebbles and look so much like a pebble it is impossible to spot them in the wild except when they flower

CACTUS
LEAVES

The sharp spines of cacti are actually leaves. They evolved over generations to protect the plant and to slow the rate of moisture loss.

Barrel cactus

CACTUS

Some people have cacti collections; they grow many varieties of the plants in heated greenhouses.

8

Right, "Jennifer Ann" orchid cacti
Above, a type of succulent commonly called "hen and chicks"

Though we associate cacti with deserts, a large family of cacti thrive in the **rain forests** of Central and South America. Called forest cacti, they are completely different in appearance from desert cacti. Growing mostly in the crotches of trees in light shade, they have flattened, or pencil-like, dangling stems. They usually lack spines. Both desert and forest cacti can display magnificent flowers—often as beautiful and as big as tropical water lilies.

CACTUS

*The crown cactus
has beautiful red
flowers and a pattern
of spines that give
the plant a silvery
appearance.*

CACTUS
HISTORY

*The rose cactus dif-
fers from most other
cacti by producing
true leaves, suggest-
ing that spiny desert
cacti evolved from
leafy plants.*

*Rose cactus filled
with pollen*

CACTI HISTORY

Cacti originated as leafy forest dwellers; most changed their form to survive in the desert. Their beginnings can be traced to Central America; from there, they spread throughout the American continent.

Prickly pear fruit

Until 65 million years ago, Earth had a climate that was mostly warm and moist. But large areas of dry deserts began to appear, and the plants that became cacti shed their leaves to cope with the drier conditions. During millions more years of **evolution**, some changed even more to return to the forest.

When Christopher Columbus brought some species of prickly pear cacti back to Europe after his exploration of North America, they spread into the dry areas of Spain and Italy.

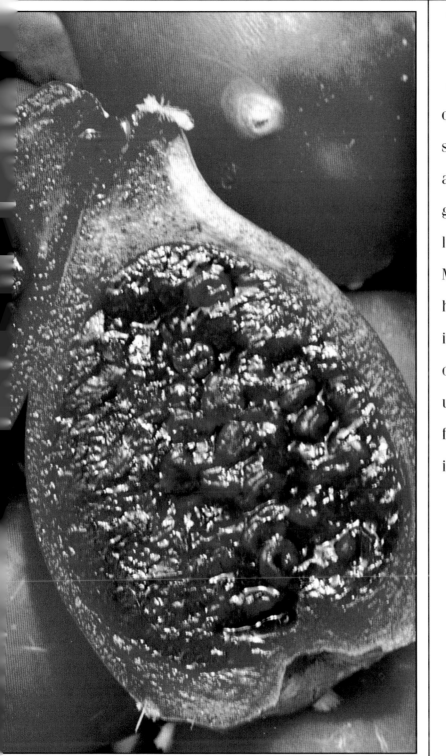

Prickly pear cacti produce large quantities of edible fruit, which are sold in supermarkets as an exotic fruit. They are grown in orchards just like apples and pears. More recently, scientists have discovered that various types of cacti have other properties that are useful in the medical field to cure illness.

The flowers of some varieties of cacti can measure 10 inches (25.4 cm) across.

Immature prickly pear fruits

Cacti grow in all shapes and sizes. The Christmas cactus and the night blooming cereus are especially unique. Both have flattened, segmented green stems that drape from the tops of trees. They draw nourishment through their roots, which dig into pockets of decayed vegetable matter in tree trunks, and from humid air through **pores** in their stems. The mistletoe cactus is closely related to the Christmas cactus. It has slender stems and produces white berries.

CACTUS
WEIRD

Sometimes the tips of immature saguaro cacti stems are damaged, causing the stems to fan out in bizarre shapes.

13

Top left, mistletoe cacti
Bottom left, "Miss Muffet" orchid cactus
Opposite, blooming sea urchin cacti

CACTUS

SHADE

Like the tropical flowers for which they were named, orchid cacti grow mostly from the shady branches of tall trees.

Right, desert cacti
Above, torch cacti

To survive the heat and drought of the desert, cacti reduced the amount of surface area exposed to the sun's harmful radiation by taking on rounded and column shapes. Examples include the barrel cactus and the saguaro cactus which grows tall columnar stems as tall as a mature oak tree. They became leafless by turning their leaves into spines to create an insulating layer close to the plant's skin. Spines are also efficient at collecting drops of fog and dew from the air and dripping it down to the plant's shallow roots.

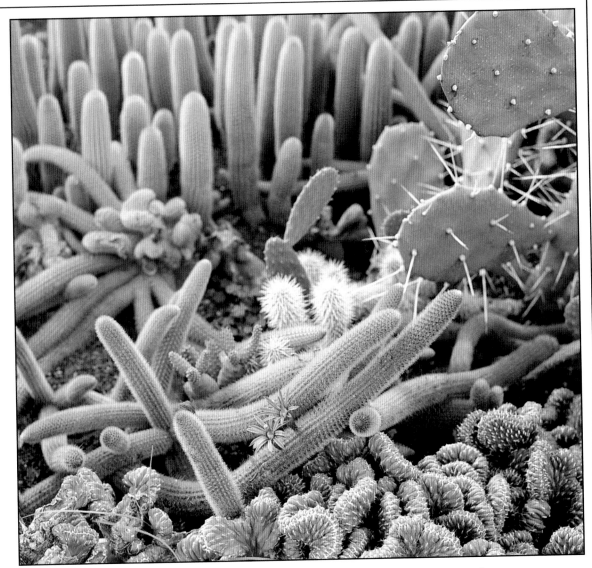

CACTUS
CARPET

*Desert cacti are **terrestrial** and can creep across the ground to form large, spreading colonies.*

CACTUS
STAR

The flowers of the star cactus resemble a waterlily. To bloom, this cactus needs winter rains.

Colony of desert cacti in a lathe house

All plants have pores through which to breathe, but in cacti they are sunken, reducing moisture loss. The cell sap of cacti is also jelly-like instead of runny, and this **viscosity** helps to retain moisture. In spite of these miraculous adaptations for survival, desert cacti are highly vulnerable to any kind of soil disturbance or climate change. They are extremely slow-growing, and a careless footstep or the wheel of an off-road vehicle can be devastating.

CACTUS
AFRICA

Lithops (a Latin word meaning "stones") resemble North American desert cacti, but they evolved in the deserts of Africa.

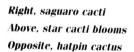

Right, saguaro cacti
Above, star cacti blooms
Opposite, hatpin cactus

Perhaps the most amazing of all desert cacti is the saguaro cactus—native to the Sonoran Desert. Just beyond the city limits of Tucson, Arizona, is the Saguaro National Forest—a stark desert wilderness filled with the strange column-like trunks of the saguaro cactus. They can reach a height of 50 feet (15.25 m), with a trunk diameter of 2.5 feet (76 cm). In Arizona, flowering occurs in June.

CACTUS

BARREL

*The most common
shape for cacti is the
barrel shape; the
color of the spines
can make them
appear yellow or red.*

**Right, Easter cactus
Above, star cactus**

Large white flowers with powdery yellow centers are clustered high up on the column tips. They are pollinated mostly by bats that are drawn to the flower in search of a sweet, sugary nectar at the base of the petals. The red, egg-shaped fruits are edible and yield a syrupy juice. Gila woodpeckers make nesting holes in the tallest columns, and owls will take over the abandoned nesting sites for their own homes.

Most desert cacti are killed by freezing temperatures. The hardiest is the northern prickly pear which grows in poor sandy and gravelly soils on rock cliffs and sand dunes as far north as Massachusetts in the Northeast and British Columbia in the Northwest. Its flattened oval pads are spiny and grow close to the ground.

In the wild, desert cacti most often germinate from seed in the shadow of a desert shrub, called a nurse plant.

Left, blooming rose pincushion cactus
Above, healthy cacti bloom continually

CACTUS
ORANGE

The cob cactus, a native of the deserts of South America, has a lovely orange blossom shaped like a starburst.

Center, barrel cacti
Above, cob cactus

CACTI NEIGHBORS

Though only cacti are part of the plant genus called Cactacaea, many other plant families have similar adaptations (such as thick stems and sharp spines) for survival in hot, dry environments. Collectively, these plants are called **succulents.** All species of cacti are succulents, but not all succulents are cacti. The family that most closely resembles desert cacti in appearance is called the Euphorbias, succulents that thrive in the deserts of Africa.

Other large plant families of succulents include Aloes (from Africa), Agaves (from the Americas) and Sedums (worldwide).

Botanical gardens often group succulents—including cacti—in greenhouse settings designed to resemble a desert **habitat.**

The Red Riding Hood cactus, named for the fairy tale character, has red petals that are displayed like a hood around a yellow center that resembles a face.

Prickly pear cactus

CACTUS
VARIETY

There are 2,000 wild species of cacti that resemble many strange forms, including a snake, a brain, a stone, and a scouring pad.

Right, Christmas cactus
Above, "Peach Monarch" cactus

In frost-free areas these collections are planted outdoors. The *Jardin Exotique*, in Monaco, on the rocky shores of the Mediterranean Sea houses such a collection. In desert communities such as Arizona and Southern California, suburban homes also use succulents to create beautiful landscapes that help to conserve water and control erosion. Any planting designed to conserve water is called a xeriscape. Cacti are also valuable because they make it possible for other forms of wildlife to exist. A wonderful example of this is at the Sonora Desert Museum.

There, desert animals live in perfect harmony, including owls and woodpeckers which nest in the burrows hollowed out of the tall saguaro cacti. Colonies of low, spreading cacti—such as the spiny serpent cactus—also provide shelter for snakes and scorpions that hide from **predators** beneath the prickly stems. Even desert-dwelling deer, with their long spindly legs and small hooves, can take refuge among the snake-like stems of serpent cacti, tip-toeing between the spiny growth, out of reach of coyotes and cougars. Cactus flowers provide nectar to feed hummingbirds, bees, bats and other **pollinators**.

CACTUS
STRAPS

Forest cacti are **epiphytic***; they have long, strap-like stems that can extend 100 feet (30.5 m) from the tops of rain forest trees.*

Some cactus flowers can measure 10 inches (25.4 cm) across

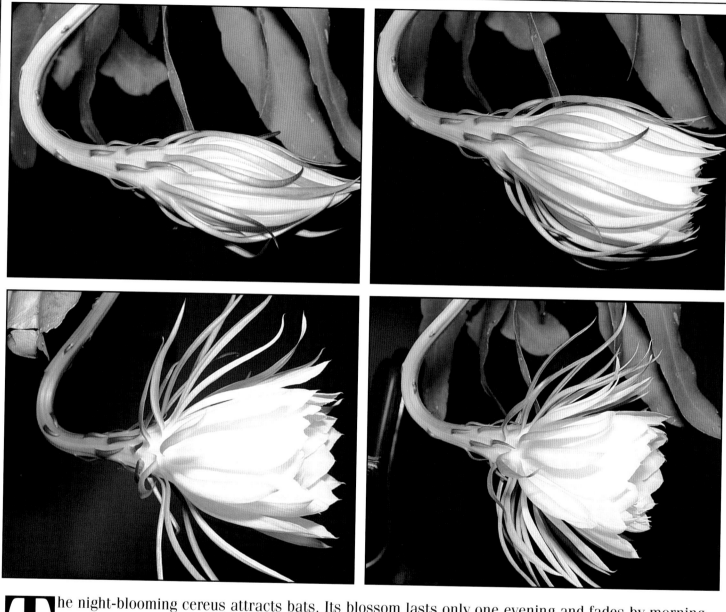

The night-blooming cereus attracts bats. Its blossom lasts only one evening and fades by morning. Once it begins to open, the petals unfold so quickly it's possible to watch and see them move. From bud to being fully open takes less than one hour. For example, at 5:00 p.m., the pointed flower bud swells up like a balloon as darkness approaches. About 15 minutes later, petals start to release themselves from the bud casing, composed of sepals (modified leaves).

At 5:30 p.m., the sepals separate from the true petals, and a pleasant perfume fills the air, attracting bats for **pollination**. Then, at 6:00 p.m., the flower is fully open, inviting pollinating bats to poke their noses into the bloom for a drink of nectar.

CACTUS
D Y E S

The ancient Aztec Indians of Central and South America once made a red dye, called cochineal, from the dried bodies of a particular insect that lives only on cactus plants.

CACTUS
C A N D L E

The limbs of the East Indian candelabrum cactus give this large plant the shape of a candelabra, or massive candle holder.

Opposite, stages of the cereus bloom
Left, fully open cereus

CACTUS
B I R D

The cactus wren, so named because it lives in holes made in cacti, is the state bird of Arizona.

Above, polka dot cacti

CACTI AS HOUSE PLANTS

Many kinds of cacti make beautiful house plants for both sunny indoor locations and shady areas. Generally speaking, all desert cacti (such as the barrel cactus) grow best in full sun, while forest cacti (which includes the Christmas cactus) prefer a lightly shaded location.

CACTUS
RITUAL

During the Papago Indians' rainmaking ritual, a special beverage made from the saguaro cactus was consumed.

CACTUS
DANGER

The bunny's ear cactus has pads that look soft and furry enough to touch, but actually its tiny needle-sharp spines can be painful and are difficult to remove from human skin.

Left and above, varieties of indoor cacti

Desert cacti can be grown from seed and from offsets. Seed forms in capsules after the flower fades. It is often quite easy to **germinate** the seed simply by placing it in a seed tray filled with a mixture of moist sand and vermiculite (a granular substance that helps retain moisture, which seeds need).

CACTUS
IMPOSTER

Many plants from the deserts of Africa resemble cacti, such as species of Euphorbia, but they are not true cacti.

Below, cinnamon cactus Right, young cacti growing in seed trays

O nce the seed is germinated and the young plant has established a root system, watering can be reduced.

As another means of **propagation**, desert cacti produce offsets—small replicas of the parent plant. These can be gently separated and moved into separate pots. Forest cacti are most easily propagated in this manner.

here the segment (called a leaf cutting) touches the soil it will produce roots and grow an exact replica of its parent. Forest cacti generally require regular amounts of watering and a peat based potting soil.

Since many kinds of cacti have spreading, or weeping, stems (such as the Christmas cactus), they can be grown in hanging baskets and window-box planters.

CACTUS
FRUITS

The fruits of the prickly pear cactus are sweet, juicy, and, when peeled, taste like blackberries.

Blooming barrel cactus

CACTUS
CHRISTMAS

The Christmas cactus grows in the rain forests of South America, where it blooms only during the winter months.

**Right, cow's horn cactus
Opposite, orchid cactus blossom**

Though both desert and forest cacti are decorative in their different forms, a bonus can be their spectacular flowers. Cacti also make spectacular garden plants in any frost-free climate. These wonders of the plant world are so versatile they can be enjoyed equally whether viewed in a natural desert or forest habitat, or kept as garden or house plants.

Glossary

Plants that live on other plants or trees are **epiphytic.**

Evolution is the gradual change that animals and plants make over many hundreds or thousands of years.

A **foraging** animal is one that survives by searching for and eating plants; deer are foraging animals.

To **germinate** is the action of a seed sprouting.

A **habitat** is a place—such as mountains, deserts, and rain forests—where particular animals and plants live.

A **lathe house** is a wooden structure composed of posts supporting a canopy of widely spaced slats to provide shade for plants, especially in their seedling stage when they are most susceptible to drying out.

Pollen are tiny powder-like particules that flowers produce in order for plants to mate and propagate by forming seed.

Pollination is the transfer of pollen grains between plants. This results in fruit formation and seed production.

A **pollinator** is any agent (a bee, a bat, even the wind) that causes the transfer of pollen.

Pores are holes in skin to allow air in and moisture out.

A predatory animal is one that survives by hunting other animals for meat; the cougar is a predatory animal, or **predator**.

Propagation among plants is any means of starting new growth—mostly by seeds, by division, and by cuttings.

A **rain forest** is a jungle that has excessive amounts of moisture, encouraging the trees to grow very tall, and sheltering a great diversity of plant and animal life.

Plants that grow in soil are **terrestrial.**

Succulent is a general term for plants with thickened leaves or stems that enable them to survive drought.

Viscosity describes thickened fluid that does not freely.

Index